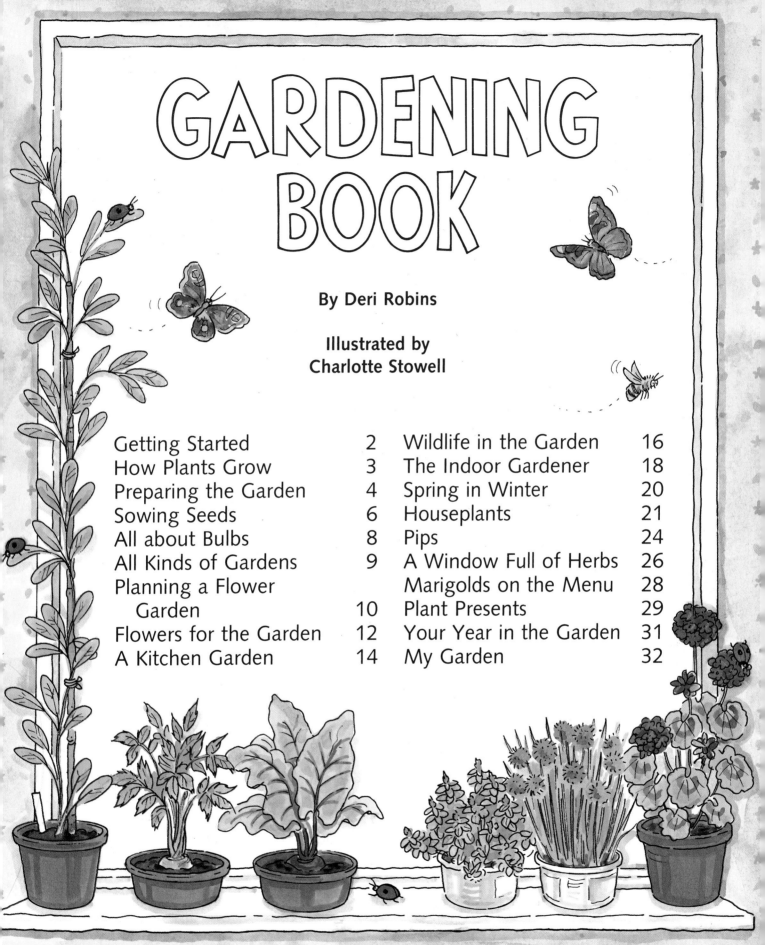

GARDENING BOOK

By Deri Robins

Illustrated by
Charlotte Stowell

Kingfisher Books

Getting Started...

You can make a garden almost anywhere – even if you only have a small balcony or a windowsill, you can fill it with an amazing variety of flowers, fruits and herbs. If you have a patch of garden outdoors, so much the better . . .

Pages 26-27

You may want to fill a windowbox with herbs . . .

Pages 10-13

Or create a beautiful flower border.

Pages 14-15

You may want to grow a saladful of vegetables . . .

Page 15

Or just keep one special tomato plant as a pet.

Whether you decide to go in for gardening in a big way . . .

. . . or just a little way . . .

. . . you'll find it's full of excitement and surprises!

First of all, you're going to need some tools.

To grow things in pots and tubs, you should be able to get by with an old fork and spoon. To grow things in the garden, you'll need to beg, borrow or buy:

A small garden spade (you can buy special junior ones)

A junior or small garden fork (for lifting out plants and breaking up hard soil)

A trowel and a hand fork
A pair of secateurs

A watering can and a pair of thick gardening gloves

A rake (for smoothing the surface of the soil)

All plants need WARMTH, LiGHT, and WATER to grow...

How Plants Grow

At first glance, you may not think that the showy azalea has much in common with the humble potato.

In fact, they have everything in common – everything they need in order to survive, that is. In the first place, *all* plants need water to grow. That's why a seed stays a seed as long as it's kept in its dry, sealed packet. As soon as it is put into some damp soil, it begins to suck in moisture and really gets going. Beneath the soil, it puts out roots to collect water and nutrients* Above the surface, shoots appear and take in carbon dioxide from the air through the leaves. This, mixed with the water and nutrients sucked in by the roots, makes the plant's food.

By the way, plants also 'breathe' out oxygen as they make their food – which, by an incredible coincidence, is what we humans need to breathe in order to live. In turn, *we* breathe out the carbon dioxide that the plants need . . .

We need each other!!

As well as food and water, plants need the warmth and light of the Sun to give them energy to make food.

Watching Seeds Grow

If you want to see how plants grow, you can grow some beans from seed. Roll up a piece of blotting paper and put it into a jam jar. Poke three or four broad bean seeds between the paper and the glass, and fill with water.

blotting paper
water
beans (seeds)

shoot
root

This way chaps!...

see Page 15

1. Start the seeds off like this . . .

2. . . . and keep the water topped up.

3. First the roots, then the shoots, appear.

4. Plant in the same way as the runner beans on page 15.

* nutrients: the minerals found in soil

Preparing the Garden

The best place for growing most outdoor plants is a sunny sheltered spot where the soil is rich and crumbly. You may not be able to choose the position of your garden, but you can do a lot about making the soil more plant-friendly.

DIGGING THE GARDEN

Digging loosens the soil so that the little seedlings can push through easily. It also helps to get rid of weeds, and gives you a chance to feed the soil with compost.

1. Dig a small trench with a spade. Push the blade down with your foot, and lift from the bottom of the handle. Pile up the soil on one side of the trench.

2. Dig another trench right next to the first one, and use the soil from this trench to fill the first one. Mix in a spadeful of compost as you do so.

3. Keep going until the whole area has been dug over in this way. Use the pile of soil from the first trench to fill the last one.

If you do this in late summer, the winter frosts will help you further by breaking down the soil ready for spring. Then all you may need to do when you come to plant your seeds or seedlings is to rake over the earth (or lightly fork over if the soil is rather hard).

WATER

Plants need plenty of water, especially during the hot summer months. As a rule, if you stick your finger in the soil and find that it's dry as far down as you can feel, it's time to give them a good soaking. Always do this in the evening.

WEEDS: THE UNINVITED GUESTS

Weeds can take over the garden and choke out your beloved plants. Learn to recognize the main offenders, and pull them up by their roots as soon as they appear. Don't wait for them to flower, or they will scatter their seeds everywhere.

vegetable peelings

leaves

grass cuttings

torn up newspaper

old plants

COMPOST

Keep a compost heap in a small area of the garden that isn't used for growing things. It looks best if you can fence it off – try winding some netting around four garden sticks. Pile in grass cuttings, vegetable peelings and dead plants – it will all rot down nicely into just the sort of food that growing plants need.

PESTS

All gardens are swarming with animals. Which are good news for your plants, and which are bad? On the whole, the slow-movers (slugs, snails, caterpillars, blackfly and greenfly) will chomp enthusiastically on leaves and growing vegetables, while the fast-movers like birds, ladybirds, frogs, toads, hoverflies and some wasps) will eat up the other lot.

If you must kill pests, don't use insecticides. Slugs and snails will crawl into a buried yoghurt pot filled with beer, and drown. Woodlice will trap themselves in a hollowed-out apple, while a hollowed-out turnip spells trouble for millipedes. Greenfly and blackfly can be given a stiff spray with soapy water. And new little plants can be protected by rings cut from a plastic bottle.

On the whole these do more GOOD than harm in the garden

...... but look out for these HORRORS!!

SOWING SEEDS

All the plants in this book grow from seeds (such as lettuces and sunflowers) or bulbs and corms (such as daffodils, crocuses and onions). You can also take cuttings from plants that are already growing (see page 22).

Before sowing seeds in the garden, you will need to prepare the soil (see page 4). Each seed packet will tell you how to sow the seeds:

• SOW BY 10/92 — Always use before the date shown

Nasturtium

USE — Where to plant the seeds

SOW — Describes the colour, height and width

AFTERCARE

Chart to show flowering time

Where to plant the seeds

How and when to plant the seeds

How to care for the growing plants

SOWING SEEDS

1. Rake the soil smooth.

2. Make a shallow trench by dragging a stick lightly across the surface.

3. Sow the seeds into the trench and cover with a *thin* layer of fine soil.

4. Mark each row with old lolly sticks.

5. Water very lightly with a watering can.

6. Make sure the shoots don't crowd each other out – pull some out gently by the leaves.

up there?.. You must be joking!!

The largest flower in the world is the Rafflesia, (also known as the parasitic stinking corpse lily). It's over a metre wide and smells HORRIBLE!!

pooh!

WEED OR SEED?

Shoots have begun to appear in the garden. Are they the real thing, or just weeds? Find out by planting a few extra seeds indoors, and compare these shoots to the ones in the garden.

You may prefer to start your seeds off indoors. This helps them to grow strongly, and makes them flower more quickly.

1. Fill a seed tray with some compost. Sprinkle the seeds over the top.

2. Cover with a thin layer of compost – no thicker than the seeds themselves – and water lightly.

3. Make a greenhouse by tying polythene over the top of the trays. Put the tray in a warm, light place. Take off the polythene when the shoots appear.

4. When each shoot is big enough to handle, dig up gently with a small stick and plant in a new tray. Leave about 5 cm between each little plant.

5. Put the trays in the garden for a few weeks. This gives them a chance to get used to the great outdoors before you plant them out in the garden.

The tallest cactus is in the Arizona Desert and is nearly 18 metres high!

all about BULBS

Bulbs (and corms, which are similar) bring many of the first flowers of the year into the garden. Delicate-looking snowdrops manage to push through the frozen soil in winter, often making a triumphant appearance while there is still snow on the ground. Next come crocuses, daffodils, bluebells, hyacinths and tulips.

The bulb is the food supply of the plant. After the flowers and leaves have died down, all the goodness goes back into the bulb so that it can grow again during the following year.

Most outdoor bulbs are planted in the garden during the autumn. Dig holes in the earth with a trowel, pop in the bulb (with the pointed end upwards) and cover with at least as much soil as the size of the bulb itself.

For a meadow-like garden, grow bulbs in the lawn! Take a handful and throw them up in the air – and plant them where they land. (Note: not all garden owners will like this idea. Check first.)

daffodil

bluebell

grape hyacinth

crocus

snowdrop

tulip

crocus

daffodil

iris

★ When your bulbs have finished flowering— let the leaves die down before you take them off.

All Kinds of Gardens

The Hanging Gardens of Babylon were one of the Seven Wonders of the World. They were built to please Nebuchadnezzar's wife, who missed her hilly homeland!

In the Middle Ages, flowers grew wild in meadows. Monks grew herbs for cooking, medicine and wine; hemp and flax were grown for rope and cloth, and indigo provided ink for manuscripts.

Tiny bonsai trees and peaceful water gardens are popular in Japan. Some gardens have no plants at all – just rocks and gravel.

During the reign of Queen Elizabeth I, gardens were laid out in formal patterns. Bushes and flowerbeds were arranged in knots and mazes, and 'statues' were cut from rosemary bushes.

The hot favourite in the Victorian parlour was the aspidistra – a gloomy-looking plant which went perfectly with the dark, heavy furniture of the time.

hic!

Planning a Flower Garden

Before you dash enthusiastically into the garden with a clutch of seed packets in your hand, spend a little time thinking about the way the different flowers will look together. How high will the plants grow? When will they flower? What colour will the flowers be? The chart on pages 12–13 will help you plan your garden.

WHAT WILL YOU GROW?

You can grow your flowers from bulbs, ready-grown plants or seeds. Flowers that grow from seed are either *annuals*, *biennials* or *perennials.* In many ways, annuals are the most fun for beginners to try. Many can be sown straight into the garden, and will produce a bright display of flowers during the year that they are sown. Biennials need to be raised in special seed beds or trays, and don't usually flower until the second year. Perennials are plants that keep growing and flowering year after year.

WHERE SHOULD YOU PLANT THEM?

Most flowers like plenty of light, but some prefer shade. Check the seed packets. Nearly all like rich soil – but nasturtiums like to rough it in poor soil. Always plant tall flowers at the back of the border, small ones near the front and the rest in between. Mix different types together, or grow in separate rows. Don't forget that many flowers will grow happily in tubs, windowboxes and hanging baskets . . .

WHEN SHOULD YOU PLANT THEM?

Most bulbs are planted in autumn to flower in the spring. Seeds are sown in spring and summer – the packets will tell you when. Try to arrange it so that plants that flower early in the year share the same part of the border as those that bloom later on.

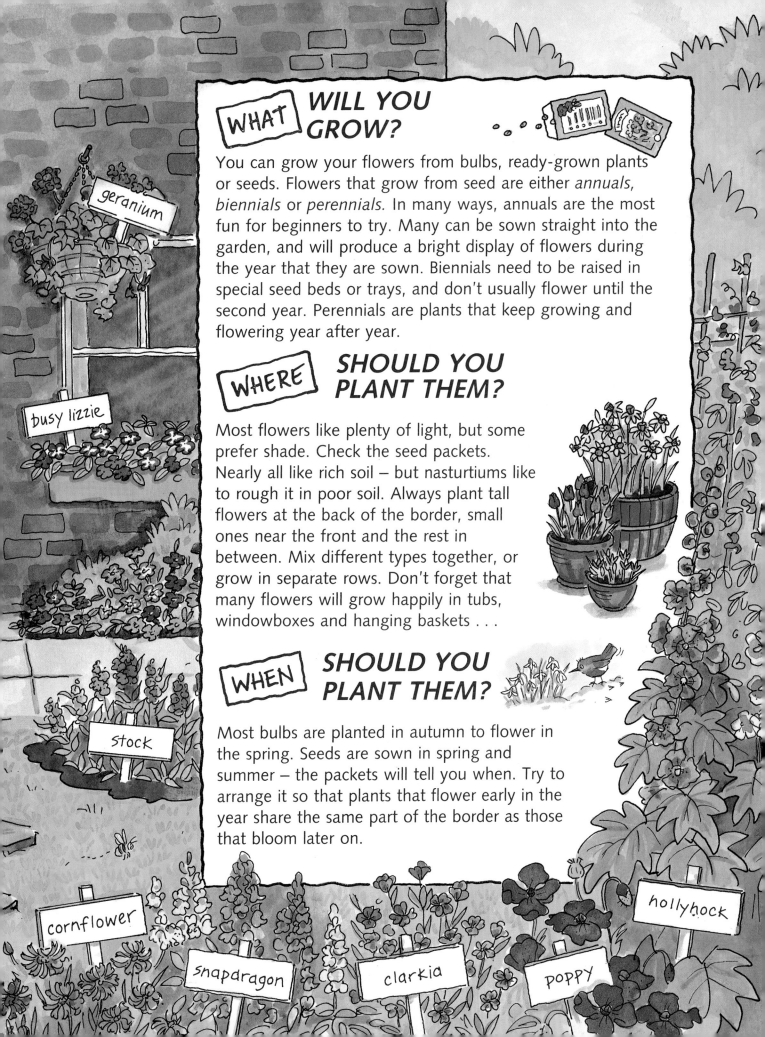

geranium

busy lizzie

stock

cornflower

snapdragon

clarkia

poppy

hollyhock

Flowers for the Garden

Here are some facts and figures about some of the most popular garden plants, starting with those that flower in early spring . . .

Name	Colour of flowers	Flowering time	Place in the garden
Crocus (corm)		Late winter to early spring	Front of border; among grass
Daffodil (bulb) !		Early to mid spring	Middle of border; among grass
Tulip (bulb)		Early to late spring	Middle of flowerbed
Pansy (biennial)		Early spring to late summer	Front of border
Marigold (annual)		Late spring to early autumn	Front of border
Lupin (perennial) !		Early to mid summer	Back of border
Busy lizzie (perennial)		Early summer to early autumn	Front of border
Snapdragon (annual)		Early summer to late autumn	Middle of border
Sweet pea (annual) !		Mid to late summer	Back of border
Stock (annual)		Early to late summer	Front of border; around gates & doors
Nasturtium (annual)		Early to late summer	Front of border, in poor soil.
Sunflower (annual)		Mid summer to early autumn	Back of border
Michaelmas daisy (perennial)		Late summer to mid autumn	Middle of border

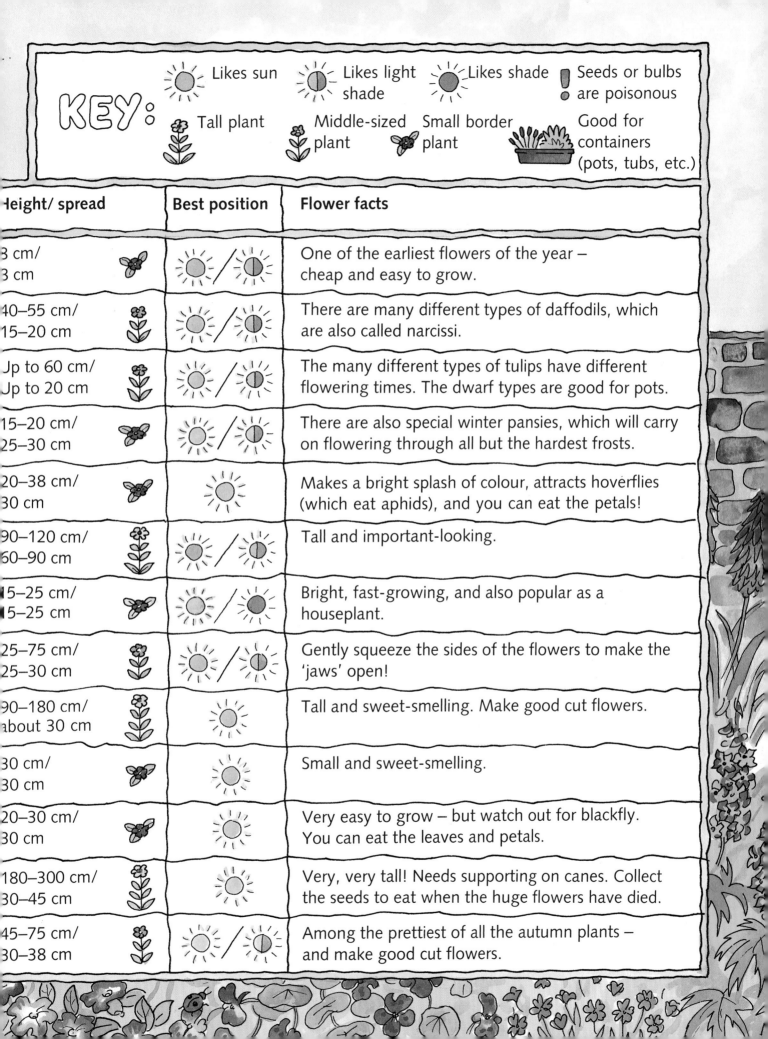

Height/ spread		Best position	Flower facts
3 cm/ 3 cm	🌼	☀ / ☀	One of the earliest flowers of the year – cheap and easy to grow.
40–55 cm/ 15–20 cm	🌼	☀ / ☀	There are many different types of daffodils, which are also called narcissi.
Up to 60 cm/ Up to 20 cm	🌼	☀ / ☀	The many different types of tulips have different flowering times. The dwarf types are good for pots.
15–20 cm/ 25–30 cm	🌼	☀ / ☀	There are also special winter pansies, which will carry on flowering through all but the hardest frosts.
20–38 cm/ 30 cm	🌼	☀	Makes a bright splash of colour, attracts hoverflies (which eat aphids), and you can eat the petals!
90–120 cm/ 60–90 cm	🌼	☀ / ☀	Tall and important-looking.
15–25 cm/ 15–25 cm	🌼	☀ / ☀	Bright, fast-growing, and also popular as a houseplant.
25–75 cm/ 25–30 cm	🌼	☀ / ☀	Gently squeeze the sides of the flowers to make the 'jaws' open!
90–180 cm/ about 30 cm	🌼	☀	Tall and sweet-smelling. Make good cut flowers.
30 cm/ 30 cm	🌼	☀	Small and sweet-smelling.
20–30 cm/ 30 cm	🌼	☀	Very easy to grow – but watch out for blackfly. You can eat the leaves and petals.
180–300 cm/ 30–45 cm	🌼	☀	Very, very tall! Needs supporting on canes. Collect the seeds to eat when the huge flowers have died.
45–75 cm/ 30–38 cm	🌼	☀ / ☀	Among the prettiest of all the autumn plants – and make good cut flowers.

A Kitchen Garden

Vegetables eaten fresh from the garden always taste special. Even if you only have a tiny flowerbed, try sneaking a few lettuces in among the marigolds — the hoverflies that buzz around this flower should keep the aphids at bay!

LETTUCES

Sow the seeds outdoors in late spring, or start off indoors in early spring. Keep them about 25–30 cm apart, and don't let the soil dry out.

Don't use up a whole packetful of seeds at once — sow some each week throughout the growing season, and you'll always have fresh ones to pick. Pick when a firm heart has formed.

SPRING ONIONS

Sow throughout spring for a summer crop. Rake the soil well before sowing — there's nothing a spring onion hates more than lumpy earth. As soon as the leaves flop over, bend them back so that the sunlight can get at the bulbs.

RADISHES

Sow throughout spring. They'll be ready a few weeks after sowing — pick them while they're still small and luscious.

CARROTS

Sow in late spring. Sow more seeds as you pull out the ripe ones (the first ones should be ripe later in the summer). Some (but not all) gardeners think that sowing onions next to carrots keeps the carrot fly away. There's no harm in trying . . .

Did you know that carrot leaves were worn as ornaments by the women in the court of Charles I . . .

. . . or that leeks were cultivated by the ancient Egyptians . . .

RUNNER BEANS

These are really fast movers – they can grow about 2 or 3 cm a day. It's best to start them off indoors during late spring, and they need to be supported with canes once they're up and growing.

They have beautiful red flowers that turn into pods, and are just as happy in a big tub or pot as they are at the back of the flowerbed. Keep picking the pods to make new ones grow.

TOMATOES IN A TUB

Like runner beans, these will grow happily on a patio or sunny balcony. Ask for the miniature (or bush) type when you buy the seeds.

1. Plant the seeds indoors as shown on page 7.

2. Plant the healthiest-looking seedlings in individual pots. Why not give some away as presents? You'll probably have more than you need.

3. When the plants start to flower, spray them with water each morning.
4. Keep them well watered, and feed once a week with tomato fertilizer (from a garden centre).

Keep them in a warm, sunny place, and water often.

5. Pick the tomatoes when they're ripe and rosy red!

The biggest potato ever grew to over 30 kg in weight! (...imagine how many chips that would make!)

Both the ancient Greeks and Romans were convinced that watercress was good for the brain!

The aubergine was grown in Europe first of all as a decoration.

Tomatoes were once called 'love apples'... it was said that if you sent one to the person you loved, they would love you back.

Marrows can grow to enormous sizes – such as the 48 kg specimen grown in 1982 in Gloucestershire, England

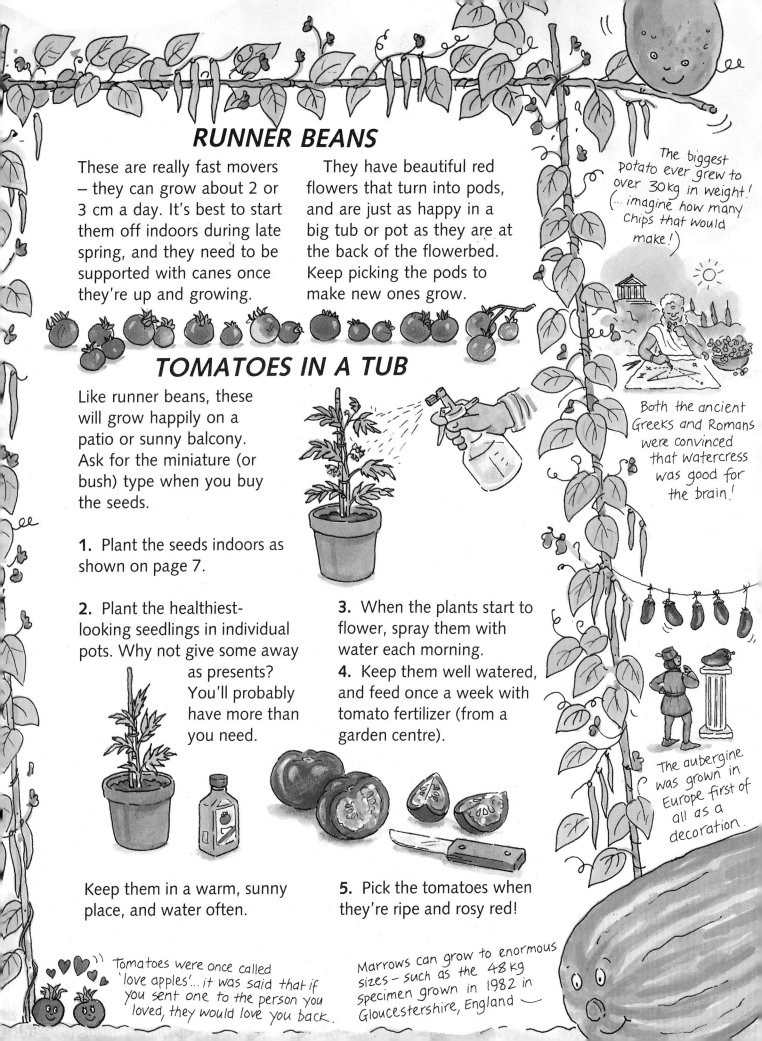

Wildlife in the Garden

Wild flowers and small animals hate neat gardens. What they love best is undisturbed countryside, where they can find plenty of food and shelter. How can you make your garden safe for wildlife without turning it into a wilderness?

MAKE HIDING PLACES

Train climbers like ivy or honeysuckle up a wall – butterflies may hang there for the winter, and birds (or even bats) may be tempted to build their nests behind the curtain of leaves. Hedgehogs may well choose to hole up in a pile of leaves and dead logs in a corner of the garden. Offer cat food if you see one – *not* milk.

DON'T MOW THE LAWN . . .

at least, not until summer. All kinds of wild flowers may appear among the grass. If the Head Gardener doesn't agree, then buy a packet of wild flower seeds from a garden centre, and sprinkle them over a well-raked corner of the flowerbed in spring or autumn.

PONDS . . .

attract toads and frogs, and provide a watering hole for passing mice and hedgehogs. Make a mini-pond by sinking a plastic bowl into the garden and filling it with water. This will be very useful to birds in the winter – they need water to bathe in to keep their feathers fluffy, which keeps their bodies warm.

DON'T POISON YOUR GARDEN

Spraying plants with insecticides kills off insect pests – but it also poisons the many useful and beautiful creatures that are good for the garden. Instead, work on attracting more of the right kinds of animals – such as hoverflies and ladybirds, which are great at gobbling up aphids. Hoverflies flock to marigolds, and ladybirds like to hibernate in the stems of teasel, fennel and cow parsley.

A BIRD TABLE . . .

will always pull in the wing-and-feather set. Put out food regularly throughout the winter – the birds will come to rely on you.

Lard or suet will attract tits, seeds and unsalted peanuts bring in the sparrows and finches, robins love grated cheese and thrushes will pounce greedily on bits of apple. Don't forget a saucer of water, and put the whole lot well away from cats. Birds will also feast on the seeds from flowerheads once the petals have died.

MEET THE MINI-BEASTS

Go on an insect safari with a magnifying glass! There are millions of tiny creatures living in the grass and under the surface – make a list of the ones you see, and look up any unfamiliar beasties in a library book . . .

the INDOOR GARDENER

Both these gardens would make lovely presents — especially the bottle garden, which hardly ever needs watering!

MINI-GARDEN

You can use any shallow container for your mini-garden — even a cardboard box will do, as long as you line it with a plastic bag:

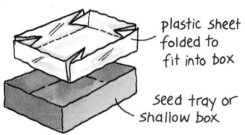

plastic sheet folded to fit into box

seed tray or shallow box

1. Line the bottom of the container with gravel or small pebbles (for drainage) and add a thin layer of charcoal (which helps to prevent moulding). Top up with potting compost — try to get the type that has sand in it, or mix in some sand yourself.

layer of charcoal
small pebbles

carrot
orange
chives

2. Press a plastic lid or bottle top into the soil, and fill with water to make a lake. Sow chive seeds around the lake.

3. Plant a lawn with grass seeds, or with mustard-and-cress. Use tiny pebbles or shells to make a

shallow plastic container to make 'lake'

pebbles + shells

compost

path, and grow 'trees' from pips — lemon, apple and orange work well. Bushy herbs like thyme make a sweet-smelling hedgerow.

4. Stock your borders with cuttings from pretty flowering pot plants — busy lizzie grows well, but it can take over the whole garden. As a final touch, tiny plastic people and animals will make your mini-garden look life-sized.

Print a 'brick wall' onto the side of your tray with a square eraser dipped into thick poster paint!

lobelia
cress
busy lizzie

GARDEN-IN-A-BOTTLE

Or, the Lazy Gardener's Garden (so-called because it hardly ever needs watering).

You will need a large, wide-necked bottle – a big sweet jar or a fishbowl both work well.

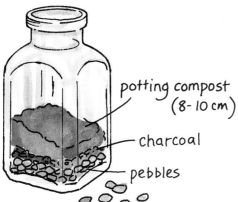

potting compost (8-10 cm)

charcoal

pebbles

1. Line the bottom of the bottle with a layer of gravel or pebbles, and top up with a layer of charcoal. Add a deep layer of potting compost. Now collect some tiny, rooted plants – ivies, ferns, mosses, and baby spider plants all work well.

Unless your bottle or jar has a really wide neck, you will need to make some special planting tools:

Spoon fixed to a piece of cane for a 'spade'

Cotton reel attached to a piece of cane to firm the soil around plants.

2. Carefully lower the cuttings into holes made by the spoon, and firm the surrounding soil with the cotton reel. Water the soil with water that has been boiled and cooled (ask an adult to do this), and put in a light place. After a few days, seal with a lid or clingfilm. The bottle should only need watering every few months.

maidenhair fern

snakeskin plant

ivy

ivy

ferns

snakeskin plants

SPRING in WINTER

It may be winter outside, but bulbs can be fooled into thinking that spring has arrived. Daffodils and hyacinths are the best ones to try – buy the type recommended for growing indoors, start them off in early autumn, and wait for the flowers to appear in the New Year. Use potting compost for daffodils, and bulb fibre for hyacinths.

1. Fill a pot with moist compost fibre. Plant the bulbs – the daffodils should have just their noses showing, while the hyacinths should be half-covered.

2. Put the pot somewhere cool and dark – *not* in a centrally-heated room. A corner of a garage or shed would be fine.

3. After a few weeks, when the shoots are growing, move the tubs out of the dark – but keep them away from direct heat.

4. When the plants look like this, they can go on a windowsill. Support tall stems with knitting needles, tying loosely with cotton.

5. Plant the bulbs out in spring, when the leaves have died. They'll probably bloom outdoors next year.

Bulbs can also flower in water. Fill a clear glass container with marbles, and stand the bulbs among them. Add enough water to cover the roots. Put in a dark place until the roots are about 10 cm long, then bring back into the light. They'll flower just as well as bulbs planted in soil, but won't be any use for planting out in the garden later on.

HOUSEPLANTS

Most houseplants are easy to grow if you follow a few simple rules . . .

Give plants the light they need. Check the label carefully, or look the plant up in a library book.

Give plants the water they need – but don't over-water, either. Give them a good soaking when the soil begins to feel dry. Add plant food to the water every week or fortnight during spring and summer.

Some plants (like palms and ferns) occasionally enjoy a lukewarm shower to clean their leaves

Spray the leaves occasionally with water – always do this in the evening.

Repot plants when they start to outgrow their containers. Gently tip the plant out of the pot, and plant in a *slightly* bigger one, surrounding it with fresh compost (see left).

Keep them in groups. They'll benefit from the moisture given off by other plants.

Don't put plants in a draughty place, OR on the TV, OR between the window and the curtains during cold weather, OR in glaring sunshine during midsummer, OR too near a radiator, OR where there is no light at all . . .

help! too hot! *help!* *help!* *help!*

FERNS
These are happiest where the air is moist and not too hot – they love bathrooms! Some are easier to keep than others – try the Boston Fern shown below.

baby spider plant

SPIDER PLANT
This has masses of green and white leaves, and puts out long snaking stems that grow baby plants. To make a new plant, cut off one of the babies and pop into fresh compost.

More ideas for indoor plants on the next page ➡

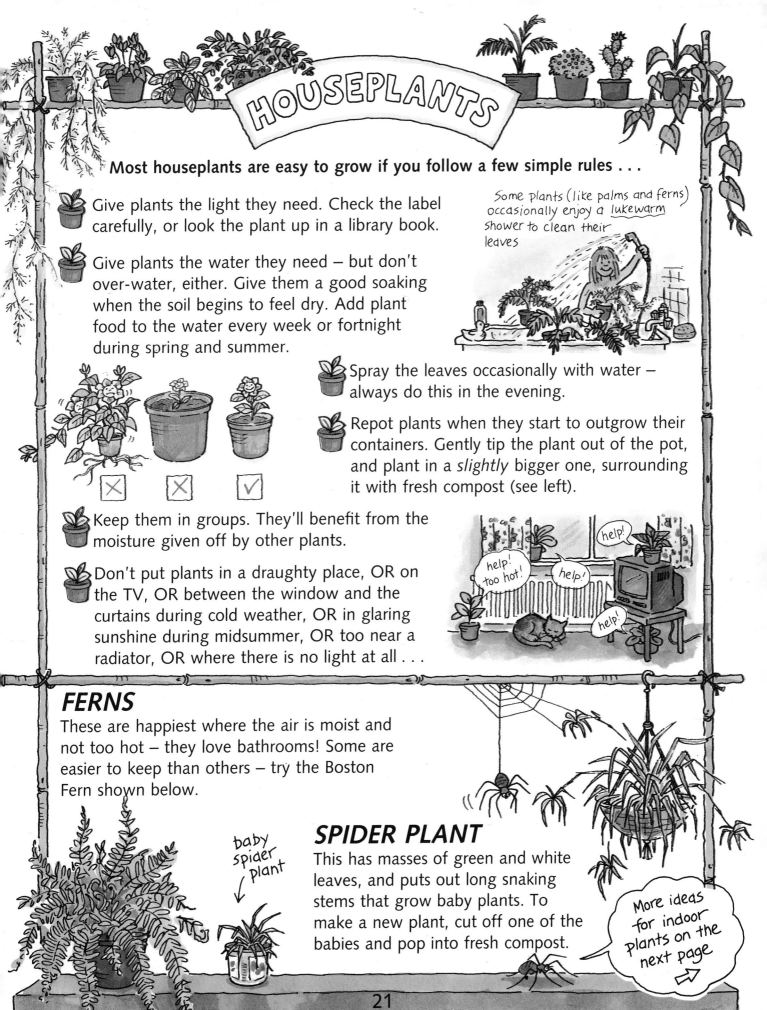

If you pinch out the growing shoot — your plant will become bushier....

TRADESCANTIA

Also known as the Inch Plant, Wandering Jew or Wandering Sailor. Grows easily from a cutting, and makes a good trailing plant.

BUSY LIZZIE

Good to grow from cuttings – your tiny shoot will quickly grow big and bushy, and will flower nearly all year round. Watch out for greenfly, though.

AFRICAN VIOLET

Always water these plants from the bottom – the velvety leaves will rot if they get wet. They prefer light shade to direct sunshine. Make new plants by sticking a leaf into fresh compost.

GERANIUM

Keep it on a sunny windowsill, and enjoy the flowers nearly all the year round! If it gets tall and leggy, snip off the top stems with scissors.

Taking Cuttings

remove lower leaves

1. Take a healthy-looking shoot from the main plant. Put the bottom 2 cm of the shoot in a glass of water.

2. When roots appear, plant the shoot in moist potting compost. Gently press the soil around the shoot, so that it supports the stem.

3. Cover with a polythene bag, and leave in a warm place away from direct sunlight for a week or so.

4. Take off the bag, and put the plant in its new home.

Plant Problems

Problem	Cause	Cure
skinny stems — small leaves	Not enough light OR needs pruning (cutting back)	Give more light OR pinch out growing shoots
lopsided growth	Only gets light on one side	Give the pot a quarter turn every other day
grows slowly.....	Underfeeding OR overwatering OR needs repotting	Feed regularly OR water less OR repot
drops buds, leaves or flowers	Sudden change of temperature or light OR in a draughty position	Put plant in a draught-free place and don't move it around
does not flower	Not enough light OR too much feeding with houseplant fertilizer	Increase light OR feed with a flowering plant fertilizer
wilting	Soil or air too dry OR overwatering OR needs repotting	Spray leaves OR water plant more moderately OR repot
brown edges on leaves	Too much direct sunlight OR air too dry OR overfeeding	Pick off dry leaves. Spray with water OR cut down feeding
yellow leaves (not wilting)	Too much lime in water or soil (if an acid-loving plant) OR needs feeding	Repot using an *acid* compost OR feed regularly
white fluff or sticky stuff on leaves....	Mealy bugs or scale insects	Scrape bugs off with a fingernail or wooden stick
'spider webs' on plant, leaves pale + mottled	Red spider mite	Keep in a warm, damp place to avoid this bug. Spray regularly with tepid water

PIPS

Little plants can be grown from all kinds of pips and stones. Some may even bear fruit one day (but they usually don't). Pips are just seeds, and are planted as shown on page 7. Most of the little plants prefer a sunny position, but don't let the soil dry out.

Oranges, lemons, tangerines, melons and pomegranates – wash and dry the seeds before you plant them.

Red, green and yellow peppers – dry the seeds, and leave for a few days before planting.

Tomatoes – wash and dry the seeds well, and put in a plastic bag for a couple of weeks before planting.

EAT ME

Plant garlic cloves in compost. Bury them about an inch deep, with the pointed ends upwards. After a couple of weeks, long narrow leaves will appear above the surface. Chop them up and add to salads, or mix with cream cheese or yoghurt . . .

Plant the top of an onion for similar-tasting leaves . . .

Carrots, beetroots and parsnip tops work too, but the leaves aren't nice to eat.

garlic   onion   carrot   parsnip   beetroot

Peanuts (not a nut at all, but a distant relation of the pea). Use the type that comes in shells, but take the shells off before planting. Don't start them off until late spring, and give them plenty of light – they'll grow quickly.

Grapes – dry the seeds, and plant several in the same pot.

Avocados, peaches and dates. Soak the hard stones in warm water overnight before planting. When the avocado starts to grow, chop it back ruthlessly or it will turn into a bare, skinny stick.

avocado

GROW A PINEAPPLE

1. Ask an adult to cut the top off a fresh pineapple for you.

2. Plant it like this:

thin layer of compost
sand (½ cm deep)
potting compost

3. Cover with a polythene bag, and leave in a slightly shady spot for 8 weeks.

4. When the leaves are growing, move to a sunny windowsill.

Your fully grown pineapple plant should look like this

peanut

pineapple

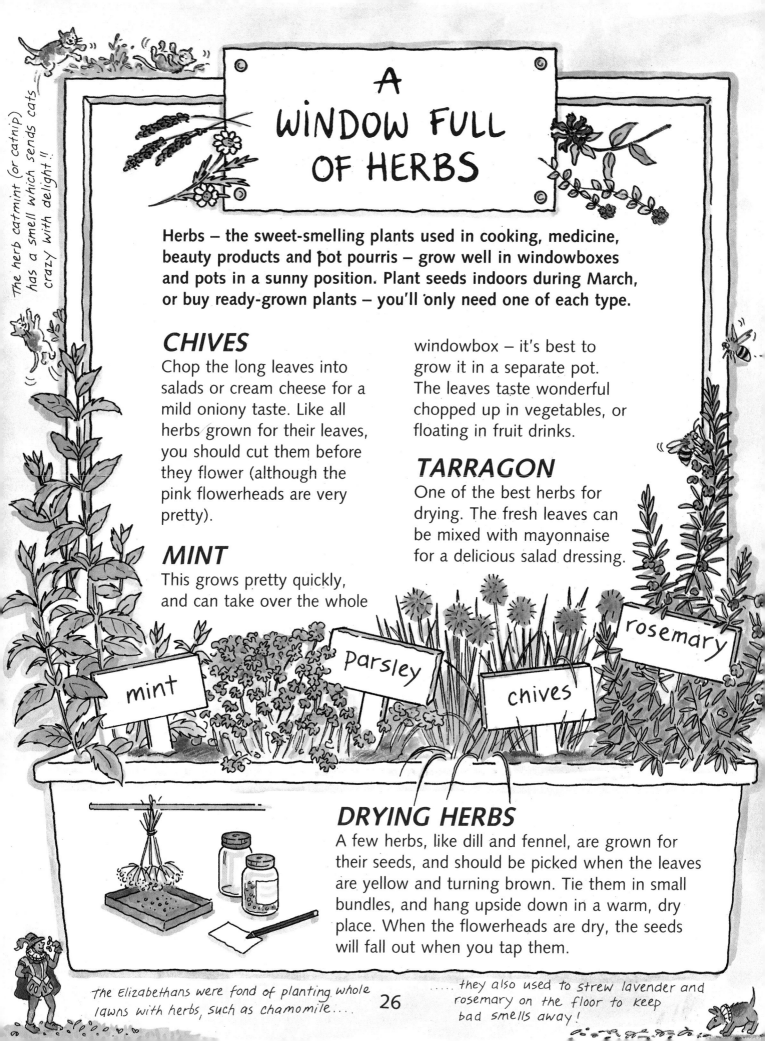

A WINDOW FULL OF HERBS

Herbs – the sweet-smelling plants used in cooking, medicine, beauty products and pot pourris – grow well in windowboxes and pots in a sunny position. Plant seeds indoors during March, or buy ready-grown plants – you'll only need one of each type.

CHIVES

Chop the long leaves into salads or cream cheese for a mild oniony taste. Like all herbs grown for their leaves, you should cut them before they flower (although the pink flowerheads are very pretty).

MINT

This grows pretty quickly, and can take over the whole windowbox – it's best to grow it in a separate pot. The leaves taste wonderful chopped up in vegetables, or floating in fruit drinks.

TARRAGON

One of the best herbs for drying. The fresh leaves can be mixed with mayonnaise for a delicious salad dressing.

DRYING HERBS

A few herbs, like dill and fennel, are grown for their seeds, and should be picked when the leaves are yellow and turning brown. Tie them in small bundles, and hang upside down in a warm, dry place. When the flowerheads are dry, the seeds will fall out when you tap them.

The herb catmint (or catnip) has a smell which sends cats crazy with delight!!

the Elizabethans were fond of planting whole lawns with herbs, such as chamomile....

..... they also used to strew lavender and rosemary on the floor to keep bad smells away!

PARSLEY

You can grow parsley all year round – bring the plant indoors during the winter.

ROSEMARY

The dark, spiky leaves of this plant keep growing all year round. It smells wonderful – bees think so, too!

LEMON BALM

Like mint, this is likely to grow at a crazy speed. The lemony leaves are nice to float in long cool summer drinks.

DILL

A soothing herb – sometimes used to make a tea to cure hiccoughs! The feathery leaves make a pretty garnish.

BASIL

Most herbs like a sunny, sheltered position, and basil is no exception. The sweet-smelling leaves go particularly well with tomatoes.

THYME

Easy to grow, and obligingly does so all year round. Smells nice and is particularly useful for stuffing meat and vegetables.

lemon balm

basil

dill

thyme

tarragon

Other herbs are grown for their stems and leaves, and should be picked before they come into flower. Hang them upside down in bunches, or spread the leaves on a tray and put in an airing cupboard to dry. Rub the brittle leaves between your finger and thumb, and store in small, airtight jars in a cool, dark place.

Fresh herbs can also be chopped and frozen in ice cube trays, then added to cooking

Most of the flowers in the garden taste awful (and some are downright poisonous) — but there are a few that really are good enough to eat.

Marigolds on the MENU

Marigold petals make a golden splash in salads — you can eat the leaves, too. The petals can also be dried and crumbled and used to turn rice and soups bright yellow. Or add a cupful of bruised petals to custard or scrambled eggs.

Nasturtiums add a peppery taste to salads and sandwiches. The buds, flowers, leaves and even the stems can be chopped finely and mixed into butter. For a pretty snack, roll a mixture of cream cheese, raisins and nuts into nasturtium leaves, and tie into a parcel with a long-stemmed flower.

Dandelions may be weeds — but the slightly bitter leaves are often used in salads. The young, tiny leaves taste best. Decorate the salad with the bright yellow flowerheads, but take these off before eating.

Rose petals can be used to make refreshing jams and jellies. The Victorians also enjoyed them on thin slices of bread spread with cream. If this doesn't appeal, try freezing tiny buds or single petals in ice cubes, for pretty drinks. Soak the buds in water for a few hours before freezing.

Plant Presents

As well as presents from the garden, you can make cards, gift tags and little pictures for framing from petals and leaves pressed between the pages of a heavy book. You could even use paper flowers cut from old seed catalogues . . .

SURPRISE SEEDS

Make a little pocket from paper, or use an ordinary envelope. Put in a handful of seeds collected from your garden, and seal down the top flap. Write clear planting instructions on the back of the envelope, without revealing the name of the flower, herb, or vegetable . . .

GROW SOMEONE'S NAME . . .

in mustard-and-cress! Cut letters from blotting paper or kitchen towel, and dampen with water. Carefully sprinkle on the seeds, so that they cover just the letters.

TINY PLANTS

Plant your spare seedlings in clay pots – paint and varnish them to look extra special.

CATMINT MOUSE

BODY

Cats go wild over catmint – grow some in a pot on the windowsill, and use some to stuff this felt mouse.

catmint

Trace off these 2 shapes.

Pin to a piece of felt, then cut them out.

BASE

END

1. Sew the body and base pieces together, and stuff with catmint.

2. Sew up the end of the mouse. Sew on ears, and sew a piece of wool to the end for a tail. Sew on beads for eyes and a nose.

EARS

glue here

squeeze together

A BATH OF HERBS

Cut circles from muslin or cotton, and fill with a handful each of sage, lavender and rose petals. Add a pinch of salt, and tie with a ribbon.

Tie herb bag around bath tap

Your Year In The Garden

SPRING

In early spring, loosen the soil with a rake and add some compost. Hardy vegetables like carrots, peas and beans can be sown in the garden in early spring. Most flowers and vegetables need to be started off indoors or sown into the garden once the frosts have passed. Check your houseplants – this is the time for repotting.

SUMMER

Keep the garden well weeded and watered as your vegetables and flowers grow. Start a compost heap in a corner of the garden. While you're enjoying your summer crops, don't forget to plant the autumn vegetables. Make sure houseplants, windowboxes and tubs don't dry out. Towards the end of summer, collect seeds from dying flowerheads.

AUTUMN

Most of your flowers and vegetables will be coming to an end. Dig up the annuals and dig over the soil, adding compost as you go. Bring tubs indoors before the frosts begin. Replace your summer annuals with autumn and winter flowers, such as pansies (which should keep going until January). Plant out bulbs to flower in the spring.

WINTER

Tidy up any trees and bushes that have become overgrown, by cutting off the ends and side branches with secateurs. Make presents and cards for Christmas from any herbs or flowers you have dried or pressed. Think about next year's garden – browse through catalogues, and send off for new seeds. Try sketching out your ideal garden!

My Garden

Name: _____   Year: _____

Address: _____   Size of garden: _____

SEEDS OR BULBS PLANTED THIS YEAR	DATE THEY WERE PLANTED	DATE THEY CAME UP	HOW WELL DID THEY DO? (TICK)		
			BRILLIANTLY	JUST OK	THEY DIDN'T

My favourite plant this year was:

_____

My biggest gardening mistake was:

_____

The thing I like best about gardening is:

_____

The thing I don't like is:

_____

Next year I am going to grow:

_____

My Dream Garden
In my dream garden, I would have:

_____
_____
_____
_____
_____

a secret hideaway

grazing animals

a water garden

Gardening consultant: Ken March
Kingfisher Books, Grisewood & Dempsey Ltd
Elsley House, 24–30 Great Titchfield Street,
London W1P 7AD
First published in 1992 by Kingfisher Books
10 9 8 7 6 5 4 3 2 1
Copyright © Grisewood & Dempsey Ltd 1992
All rights reserved.
British Library Cataloguing In Publication Data
A catalogue record for this book is available
from the British Library.
ISBN 0 86272 878 9   Printed in Spain